Prayer Book *for* Spouses

All booklets are published thanks to the generous support of the members of the Catholic Truth Society

CATHOLIC TRUTH SOCIETY
PUBLISHERS TO THE HOLY SEE

Contents

Contents

 First published 2009 by The Incorporated Catholic Truth Society, 40-46 Harleyford Road, London SE11 5AY Tel: 020 7640 0042 Fax: 020 7640 0046.

ISBN 978 1 86082 617 7

The need to pray

God has blessed the love of married people from the beginning. The Lord Jesus refined and raised up this love with a special gift of grace and charity which is conferred on the couple on the day of their marriage. Praying together will help the couple to preserve and enrich that highest of values, their love, in their marriage.

Lord, may they both praise you when they are happy and turn to you in their sorrows.
May they be glad that you help them in their work
and know that you are with them in their need.
May they pray to you in the community
of the Church,
and be your witnesses in the world.
May they reach old age in the company
of their friends,
and come at last to the kingdom of heaven.
We ask this through Christ our Lord. Amen.[1]

Prayer of Engaged Couples

Engaged couples will want to ask the blessing of God at this important stage of their lives. They will want to prepare themselves for their wedding, and pray that their love may grow in the light and strength of the love Christ has for his Church: the love of which the sacrament of marriage will be the sign.

Father, in my heart love has come alive for a person you made, and whom you too know and love. It was you who brought me to meet her (him) and come to know her (him), as once, in paradise, you brought Eve and Adam together so that man should not remain alone. I thank you for this gift. It fills me with profound joy. It makes me like you, who are love itself, and brings me to understand the value of the life you have given me.

Help me not to squander the riches you have stored in my heart. Teach me that love is a gift that must not be suffocated by selfishness; that love is pure and strong and must not be soiled or corrupted; that love is fruitful and should, beginning even now, open up a new life for myself and the person who has chosen me.

Loving Father, I pray for the person who is thinking of me and waiting for me, and who has placed in me complete trust for the future; I pray for this person who will walk along the path of life with me; help us to be worthy of one another and to be an encouragement and example to one another. Help us to prepare for marriage, for its grandeur and for its responsibilities, so that the love which fills us body and spirit may rule our lives for evermore. Through Christ our Lord. Amen.

Approaching marriage

As you know, you are about to enter into a union which is most sacred and most serious, a union which was established by God himself. By it he gave man a share in the greatest work of creation, the work of the continuation of the human race. And in this way he sanctified human love and enabled man and woman to help each other live as children of God, by sharing a common life under his fatherly care.

Because God himself is thus its author, marriage is of its very nature a holy institution, requiring of those who enter into it a complete and unreserved giving of self. But Christ our Lord added to the holiness of marriage an even deeper meaning and a higher beauty. He referred to the love of marriage to describe his own love for his Church, that is, for the people of God whom he redeemed by his own blood. And so he gave to Christians a new vision of what married life ought to be, a life of self-sacrificing love like his own. It is for this reason that his apostle, St Paul, clearly states that marriage is now and for all times to be considered a great mystery, intimately bound up with the supernatural union of Christ and the Church, which union is also to be its pattern.

The union is most serious, because it will bind you together for life in a relationship so close and so intimate that it will profoundly influence your whole future. That future, with its hopes and disappointments, its successes and its failures, its pleasures and its pains, its joys and its sorrows, is hidden from your eyes. You know that these elements are mingled in every life and are to be expected in your own. And so, not knowing what is before you, you take each other for better or worse, for richer or for poorer, in sickness and in health, until death.

Truly, then, these words are most serious. It is a beautiful tribute to your undoubted faith in each other, that, recognizing their full import, you are nevertheless so willing and ready to pronounce them. And because these words involve such solemn obligations, it is most fitting that you rest the security of your wedded life upon the great principle of self-sacrifice. And so you begin your married life by the voluntary and complete surrender of your individual lives in the interest of that deeper and wider life which you are to have in common. Henceforth, you belong entirely to each other; you will be one in mind, one in heart, and one in affections.

And whatever sacrifices you may hereafter be required to make to preserve this common life, always make them generously. Sacrifice is usually difficult and irksome. Only love can make it easy, and perfect love can make it a joy. We are willing to give in proportion as we love. And when love is perfect, the sacrifice is complete. God so loved the world that he gave his only begotten Son and the Son so loved us that he gave himself for our salvation. "Greater love than this no one has, that one lay down his life for his friends."

No greater blessing can come to your married life than pure conjugal love, loyal and true to the end. May, then, this love with which you join your hands and hearts today never fail, but grow deeper and stronger as the years go on. And if true love and the unselfish spirit of perfect sacrifice guide your every action, you can expect the greatest measure of earthly happiness that may be allotted to man in this vale of tears. The rest is in the hands of God. Nor will God be wanting to your needs; he will pledge you the life-long support of his graces in the holy sacrament which you are now going to receive.[2]

The domestic church

In virtue of the sacrament of Matrimony by which they signify and share (cf. *Eph* 5:32) the mystery of the unity and faithful love between Christ and the Church, Christian married couples help one another to attain holiness in their married life and in the rearing of their children. Hence by reason of their state in life and of their position they have their own gifts in the People of God (cf. 1 *Cor* 7:7). From the marriage of Christians there comes the family in which new citizens of human society are born and, by the grace of the Holy Spirit in Baptism, those are made children of God so that the People of God may be perpetuated throughout the centuries. In what might be regarded as the domestic Church, the parents, by word and example are the first heralds of the faith with regard to their children. They must foster the vocation which is

strengthened by so many and such great means of salvation, all the faithful, whatever their condition or state — though each in his own way — are called by the Lord to that perfection of sanctity by which the Father himself is perfect.[3]

Love one another

I give you a new commandment:
Love one another;
Just as I have loved you,
You must also love one another.
By this love you have for one another,
Everyone will know that you are my disciples.
(*John* 13:34-35)

Recalling our Promises

Bond of marriage

Father, in the great mystery of your love you have consecrated the bond of marriage as a symbol of Christ's union with his Church. May our lives give witness to the sacrament we celebrate in faith. Through Christ our Lord. Amen.[4]

Freedom

We are ready freely and without reservation to give ourselves to each other in marriage.
We are ready to love and honour each other
as man and wife for the rest of our lives.
We are ready to accept children lovingly from God
and to bring them up according to the law of
Christ and his Church.[5]

Consent

I take you for my lawful husband (wife), according to the rite of our holy Mother the Church.

I take you to be my lawful wedded husband (wife) to have and to hold from this day forward, for better for worse, for richer for poorer, in sickness and in health, to love and to cherish till death us do part.

We have declared our consent before the Church. May the Lord in his goodness strengthen our consent and fill us both with his blessings. What God has joined together, let no man put asunder.[6]

Blessing and rings

May the Lord bless these rings which we give each other as a sign of our love and fidelity. May the Lord bless and consecrate us in our love for each other. Grant that we who wear these rings may always have a deep faith in each other. May we do God's will and always live together in peace, good will and love. Through Christ our Lord. Amen.

Take this ring as a sign of my love and fidelity, in the name of the Father and of the Son and of the Holy Spirit. Amen.[7]

Nuptial Blessing

Father, by your power you have made
everything out of nothing.
In the beginning you created the universe
and made mankind in your own likeness.

You gave man the constant help of woman
so that man and woman should no longer be two,
but one flesh,
and you teach us that what you have united
may never be divided.

Father, you have made the union of man and wife
so holy a mystery
that it symbolizes the marriage of Christ
and his Church.
Father, by your plan man and woman are united,
and married life has been established
as the one blessing that was not forfeited by
original sin
or washed away in the flood.
Look with love upon this woman, your daughter,
now joined to her husband in marriage.
She asks your blessing.
Give her the grace of love and peace.

May she always follow the example
of the holy women
whose praises are sung in the scriptures

May her husband put his trust in her
and recognize that she is his equal
and the heir with him to the life of grace.

May he always honour her and love her
as Christ loves his bride, the Church.

Father, keep them always true
to your commandments.
Keep them faithful in marriage
and let them be living examples of Christian life.

Give them the strength which comes
from the gospel
so that they may be witnesses of Christ to others.
Bless them with children
and help them to be good parents.
May they live to see their children's children.
And, after a happy old age,
grant them fullness of life with the saints
in the kingdom of heaven.
We ask this through Christ our Lord.
Amen.[8]

Indissolubility

The intimate partnership of married life and love has been established by the Creator and qualified by His laws, and is rooted in the conjugal covenant of irrevocable personal consent. Hence by that human act whereby spouses mutually bestow and accept each other a relationship arises which by divine will and in the eyes of society too is a lasting one.[9]

Children

By their very nature, the institution of matrimony itself and conjugal love are ordained for the procreation and education of children, and find in them their ultimate crown. Thus a man and a woman, who by their compact of conjugal love "are no longer two, but one flesh" (*Mt* 19:6), render mutual help and service to each other through an intimate union of their persons and of their actions. Through this union they experience the meaning of their oneness and attain to it with growing perfection day by day. As a mutual gift of two persons, this intimate union and the good of the children impose total fidelity on the spouses and argue for an unbreakable oneness between them.[10]

Love and marriage

Christ the Lord abundantly blessed this many-faceted love, welling up as it does from the fountain of divine love and structured as it is on the model of His union with His Church. For as God of old made Himself present to His people through a covenant of love and fidelity, so now the Saviour of people and the Spouse of the Church comes into the lives of married Christians through the sacrament of matrimony. He abides with them thereafter so that just as He loved the Church and handed Himself over on her behalf, the spouses may love each other with perpetual fidelity through mutual self-bestowal.[11]

Human love

The biblical Word of God several times urges the betrothed and the married to nourish and develop their wedlock by pure conjugal love and undivided affection. Many people of our own age also highly regard true love between husband and wife as it manifests itself in a variety of ways depending on the worthy customs of various peoples and times.

This love is an eminently human one since it is directed from one person to another through an affection of the will; it involves the good of the whole person, and therefore can enrich the expressions of body and mind with a unique dignity, ennobling these expressions as special ingredients and signs of the friendship distinctive of marriage. This love God has judged worthy of special gifts, healing, perfecting and exalting gifts of grace and of charity. Such love, merging the human with the divine, leads the spouses to a free and mutual gift of themselves, a gift providing itself by gentle affection and by deed; such love pervades the whole of their lives: indeed by its busy generosity it grows better and grows greater. Therefore it far excels mere erotic inclination, which, selfishly pursued, soon enough fades wretchedly away.[12]

One in heart and mind

Holy Father, you created mankind in your own image and made man and woman to be joined as husband and wife in union of body and heart and so fulfill their mission in this world.

Father, to reveal the plan of your love,you made the union of husband and wife an image of the covenant between you and your people.

In the fulfillment of this sacrament, the marriage of Christian man and woman is a sign of the marriage between Christ and the Church. Father, stretch out your hand, and bless them both.

Lord, grant that as they begin to live this sacrament they may share with each other the gifts of your love and become one in heart and mind as witnesses to your presence in their marriage. Help them to create a home together and give them children to be formed by the gospel and to have a place in your family.

Give your blessings to your daughter, so that she may be a good wife and mother, caring for the home, faithful in love for her husband, generous and kind. Give your blessings to your son, so that he may be a faithful husband and a good father.

Father, grant that as they come together to your table on earth, so they may one day have the joy of sharing your feast in heaven. We ask this through Christ our Lord. Amen.[13]

Open to Life Together

Loving new life

O Immaculate Virgin, Mother of the true God and Mother of the Church, grant to our homes the grace of loving and respecting life in its beginnings, with the same love with which you conceived in your womb the life of the Son of God. Blessed Virgin Mary, protect our families, so that they may always be united, and bless the upbringing of our children.

Our hope, look upon us with compassion, teach us to go continually to Jesus and, if we fall, help us to rise again, to return to him, by means of the confession of our faults and sins in the Sacrament of Penance, which gives peace to the soul. We beg you to grant us a great love for all the holy Sacraments, which are, as it were, the signs that your Son left us on earth.[14]

Prayer before making love

Father, send your Holy Spirit into our hearts. Place within us love that truly gives, tenderness that truly unites, self-offering that tells the truth and does not deceive, forgiveness that truly receives, loving physical union that welcomes. Open our hearts to you, to each other and to the goodness of your will.

Cover our poverty in the richness of your mercy and forgiveness. Clothe us in our true dignity and take to yourself our shared aspirations, for your glory, for ever and ever. Mary, our Mother, intercede for us. Amen.

Prayer to have a child

God our Father, all parenthood comes from you. Allow us to share in that power which is yours alone, and let us see in the child you send us a living sign of your presence in our home. Bless our love and make it fruitful so that a new voice may join ours in praise of you, a new heart love you, and a new life bear witness to you. Amen.

Prayer for openness

Father, you desire so much for us. Your plan for our happiness far exceeds any dream or hope we could ever think of on our own.

We ask you Father, to open our hearts to receive your ambition for our marriage.

May we overcome any resistance we might have, such as fear of failing or of being rejected, feeling unworthy or hopeless. We ask this through Christ our Lord, Amen.[15]

Prayer for trust

Father, we praise you for your goodness. Thank you for bringing us together and for supporting us in our marriage. Help us to trust. Help us to overcome any barriers to trusting each other. Give us courage, compassion, hope, wisdom and persistence. Give us an open heart so that we might truly hear and see the pain that our spouse is experiencing and have the courage of self-sacrificing love to ease their burdens. We ask this through Jesus, our Lord. Amen.[16]

Prayer of Tobias and Sarah

The Book of Tobit recounts the story of this young couple. Their love is guided by God's angel Raphael, and protected from the demons through prayer - seen in the messianic symbol of the heart of the fish. Christian couples are encouraged to surround their love making in prayer and gratitude.

When they had finished eating and drinking and it seemed time to go to bed, the young man was taken from the dining room to the bedroom. Tobias remembered Raphael's advice; he went to his bag, took the fish's heart and liver out of it and put some on the burning incense. The reek of the fish distressed the demon, who fled through the air to

Egypt. Raphael pursued him there, and bound and shackled him at once.

The parents meanwhile had gone out and shut the door behind them. Tobias rose from the bed, and said to Sarah, 'Get up, my sister! You and I must pray and petition our Lord to win his grace and his protection.' She stood up, and they began praying for protection, and this was how he began:

You are blessed, O God of our fathers;
blessed, too, is your name for ever and ever.
Let the heavens bless you
and all things you have made for evermore.
It was you who created Adam,
you who created Eve his wife
to be his help and support;
and from these two the human race was born.
It was you who said,
"It is not good that the man should be alone;
let us make him a helpmate like himself".
And so I do not take my sister
for any lustful motive;
I do it in singleness of heart.
Be kind enough to have pity on her and on me
and bring us to old age together.
And together they said, 'Amen, Amen',
and lay down for the night.[17]

The couple's happiness

You are blessed, my God, with every blessing that is pure; may you be blessed for evermore! You are blessed for having made me glad. What I feared has not happened; instead you have treated us with mercy beyond all measure.

You are blessed for taking pity on this only son, this only daughter. Grant them, Master, your grace and your protection; let them live out their lives in happiness and in grace.[18]

Song of the Bride

Let him kiss me with the kisses of his mouth.
Your love is more delightful than wine;
delicate is the fragrance of your perfume,
your name is an oil poured out,
and that is why the maidens love you.
Draw me in your footsteps, let us run.
The King has brought me into his rooms;
you will be our joy and our gladness.
We shall praise your love above wine;
how right it is to love you.

How beautiful you are, my Beloved,
and how delightful!

His left arm is under my head,
his right embraces me.

My Beloved lifts up his voice,
he says to me,
'Come then, my love,
my lovely one, come.
For see, winter is past,
the rains are over and gone.
The flowers appear on the earth.
The season of glad songs has come,
the cooing of the turtledove is heard
in our land.
The fig tree is forming its first figs
and the blossoming vines give out their fragrance.
Come then, my love,
my lovely one, come.

My dove, hiding in the clefts of the rock,
in the coverts of the cliff,
show me your face,
let me hear your voice;
for your voice is sweet
and your face is beautiful.'[19]

Song of the Bridegroom

Come from Lebanon, my promised bride,
come from Lebanon, come on your way.
You ravish my heart,
my sister, my promised bride,
you ravish my heart
with a single one of your glances,
with one single pearl of your necklace.
What spells lie in your love,
my sister, my promised bride!
How delicious is your love,
more delicious than wine!
How fragrant your perfumes,
more fragrant than all other spices!
Your lips, my promised one,
distil wild honey.
Honey and milk are under your tongue;
and the scent of your garments
is like the scent of Lebanon.
Set me like a seal on your heart,
like a seal on your arm.
For love is strong as death,
jealousy relentless as Sheol.
The flash of it is a flash of fire,
a flame of the LORD himself.
Love no flood can quench, no torrents drown.[20]

Expecting a child

Father, we thank you for your marvellous gift; you have allowed us to share in your divine parenthood. During this time of waiting, we ask you to protect and nurture these first mysterious stirrings of life. May our child come safely into the light of the world and to the new birth of baptism. Mother of God, we entrust our child to your loving heart. Amen.

After the birth of a child

Father, we thank you with all our heart for the child you have given us. We consecrate him (her) to you; let us remember he (she) is yours as well as ours. Help us to bring up our child to be a source of your blessing. Amen.

Children: gift of marriage

Marriage and conjugal love are by their nature ordained toward the begetting and educating of children. Children are really the supreme gift of marriage and contribute very substantially to the welfare of their parents. The God Himself Who said, "it is not good for man to be alone" (*Gn* 2:18) and "Who made man from the beginning male and female" (*Mt* 19:4), wishing to share with man a certain special participation in His own creative work, blessed male and female, saying: "Increase and multiply" (*Gn* 1:28). Hence, while not making the other purposes of matrimony of less account, the true practice of conjugal love, and the whole meaning of the family life which results from it, have this aim: that the couple be ready with stout hearts to cooperate with the love of the Creator and the Saviour, Who through them will enlarge and enrich His own family day by day.[21]

Transmission of life

For God, the Lord of life, has conferred on people the surpassing ministry of safeguarding life in a manner which is worthy of man. Therefore from the moment of its conception life must be guarded with the greatest care while abortion and infanticide are unspeakable crimes. The sexual characteristics of man and the human faculty of reproduction wonderfully exceed the dispositions of lower forms of life. Hence the acts themselves which are proper to conjugal love and which are exercised in accord with genuine human dignity must be honoured with great reverence. Hence when there is question of harmonising conjugal love with the responsible transmission of life, the moral aspects of any procedure does not depend solely on sincere intentions or on an evaluation of motives, but must be determined by objective standards. These, based on the nature of the human person and his acts, preserve the full sense of mutual self-giving and human procreation in the context of true love. Such a goal cannot be achieved unless the virtue of conjugal chastity is sincerely practised.

Relying on these principles, sons of the Church may not undertake methods of birth control which are found blameworthy by the teaching authority of the Church in its unfolding of the divine law. All should be persuaded that human life and the task of transmitting it are not realities bound up with this world alone. Hence they cannot be measured or perceived only in terms of it, but always have a bearing on the eternal destiny of human beings.[22]

What is love?

Love is always patient and kind; it is never jealous; love is never boastful or conceited; it is never rude or selfish; it does not take offence, and is not resentful. Love takes no pleasure in other people's sins but delights in the truth; it is always ready to excuse, to trust, to hope, and to endure whatever comes. Love does not come to an end. (1 *Cor* 13:4-8)

Prayers of a Married Couple

Remember us today

Father, all-powerful and eternal God, we give you thanks and bless your holy name. You created mankind as man and woman and blessed their union, making them a help and support for each other. Remember us today. Look kindly on us and grant that our love may be completely unselfish, a gift like that of Christ to his Church. May we live many years together in joy and peace, and may we always give you heartfelt praise through your Son and in the Holy Spirit. Amen.

Teach us to love

Father, you called us to found this family together. Give us the grace to animate it with your love: may our family always comfort those who live in it and welcome those who enter it. Teach us to make progress in your sight through our love for each other, to do your will all the days of our life, to submit our plans to you, to ask your help, to offer you our joys and sorrows, and to lead to you the children you give us. Lord, you are Love; we thank you for our love. We ask this through Christ our Lord. Amen.

Prayer of dedication of newly married couple to the Precious Blood

Lord Jesus, we thank you for the joy of our wedding. Through all the years of our life you have watched over us to bring us together in holy Christian marriage. Lord, bless us, for we are united in love of you and of each other. Redeemed by your Precious Blood and strengthened by your grace, may we live in kindness and fidelity, in unfailing trust and love so that our whole life may be pleasing to you.

Mary, who with Joseph made a happy home at Nazareth for Jesus, take us into your motherly care. You who showed concern for a newly married couple at Cana, help and us. May our union on earth lead to that eternal union in which all the blessed will be joined together, praising the Redeeming Blood of Jesus, the Lord. Amen.[23]

Prayer for spousal unity

O God, by your power you have made everything out of nothing.

In the beginning you created the universe and made us in your own likeness.

You gave man the constant help of woman so that man and woman should no longer be two, but one flesh, and you teach us that what you have united may never be divided.

Lord Jesus, look with love upon us in our life together as husband and wife.

We ask your blessing to live with each other in peace and harmony.

May we always bear with one another's weaknesses and grow from each other's strengths.

Help us to forgive one another's failings and grant us patience, kindness, cheerfulness and the spirit of placing the well-being of one another ahead of self.

May the love that brought us together grow and mature with each passing year.

Bring us both ever closer to you through our love for each other. We ask this through Christ our Lord. Amen.

Gratitude and trust

We thank you, O God, for the love you have implanted in our hearts.

May it always inspire us to be kind in our words, considerate of feelings, and concerned for each other's needs and wishes. Help us to be understanding and forgiving of our human imperfection.

Increase our faith and trust in you and may Your Prudence guide our life and love.

Bless our marriage O God, with peace and happiness, and make our love fruitful for your glory and our joy, both here and in eternity.[24]

Wedding anniversary

Lord, our God and Father, in the beginning you created man and woman to be united in the bond of marriage. Bless and strengthen our love that our life together may be an ever truer reflection of the union between Christ and his Church. Through Christ our Lord. Amen.

Silver wedding

Father, you united us in the bond of marriage and you have sustained us through the joys and sorrows of our life together. After these many years of life together, increase and deepen our love by the power of your Spirit so that we (and our children) may always enjoy your friendship. Through Christ our Lord. Amen.

Golden wedding

God our Father, we look back today with gratitude to the time when you first blessed our love. After fifty years of life together, we pray with confidence that we may be blessed ever more fully with the rich gifts of your love. Through Christ our Lord. Amen.

Prayer for Anointing

When we sin, we not only hurt each other, we damage our unique sacramental identity which hurts the Church. We pray for deep reconciliation as one, in recognition that we are the Body of Christ.

Heavenly Father, I have failed to love my beloved (*name*) the way you trusted me to do. I regret with all my heart the pain I have inflicted and the damage I have done by not living out the promise of my wedding vows more fully. Accept my sorrow, forgive me for my sins, and grant me the grace to sin no more. Instill in me a firm conviction to love more generously, to resist self pity, and to affirm constantly the goodness of this (man/woman) whom you have given me to love.

Wife: Lord, I praise you for the gift of sexuality, of my femininity which draws me beyond myself and calls me into this wonderful union with another. I thank you for my spouse, this man that you have created and for the life we share together.

Husband: Loving God, Father, and Son, and Holy Spirit, we praise you for the love we share together. You created us in love to share in your divine life. Love is our origin, love is our constant calling, love will be our fulfilment in heaven. In our sacrament of marriage, the love we share and the home we create makes your creative love present in the world.

Wife: Merciful God, forgive us for the ways in which we have failed to love. Open our eyes to see the hurt we have done. Soften our hearts that we may truly seek forgiveness. Grace us with your mercy that we may forgive each other. Heal us. Touch our hearts that we may love again. Restore to us the unity that we have shattered.

Husband: Lord, let your healing power touch the darkest reaches of our hearts. Renew our love, that we may become one in mind and heart and grow in passion for each other. Give us a new heart, that in our love for each other we may reflect the love you have for each of us, and that together, we may be witnesses of your love for the world.

Spouses: Let us pray. Lord, you created us to love, and gift us with each other and the love that draws us together. When our love is imperfect and we hurt each other, you give us the power to forgive and heal each other. Help us to be more loving, more forgiving. Heal the hurts that continue to keep us apart, and help us always to celebrate the love we share. We make this prayer through Christ our Lord, Amen.[25]

Your spouse's faith

Oh yes, my God, I must have it, You must have it, this straight, true soul; he must know You and love You, become the humble instrument of Your glory, and do the work of an apostle. Take him entirely to Yourself. Make of my trials, my sufferings and my renunciations the road by which You will come to this dear heart. Is there anything that belongs to me alone that I would not be ready to offer You to obtain this conversion, this grace so longed for? My sweet Saviour, between Your Heart and mine there must be this compact of love, which will give You a soul and will give me for eternity him whom I cherish, whom I want to be with me in Your Heaven.[26]

The four essential qualities of married love

Personal union

This love is above all fully human, a compound of sense and spirit. It is not, then, merely a question of natural instinct or emotional drive. It is also, and above all, an act of the free will, whose trust is such that it is meant not only to survive the joys and sorrows of daily life, but also to grow, so that husband and wife become in a way one heart and one soul, and together attain their human fulfillment.

It is a love which is total — that very special form of personal friendship in which husband and wife generously share everything, allowing no unreasonable exceptions and not thinking solely of their own convenience.[27]

Indissoluble

Whoever really loves his partner loves not only for what he receives, but loves that partner for the partner's own sake, content to be able to enrich the other with the gift of himself.

Married love is also faithful and exclusive of all other, and this until death. This is how husband and wife understood it on the day on which, fully aware of what they were doing, they freely vowed themselves to one another in marriage.[28]

Faithful

Though this fidelity of husband and wife sometimes presents difficulties, no one has the right to assert that it is impossible; it is, on the contrary, always honorable and meritorious. The example of countless married couples proves not only that fidelity is in accord with the nature of marriage, but also that it is the source of profound and enduring happiness.[29]

Open to fertility

Finally, this love is fecund. It is not confined wholly to the loving interchange of husband and wife; it also contrives to go beyond this to bring new life into being. Marriage and conjugal love are by their nature ordained toward the procreation and education of children. Children are really the supreme gift of marriage and contribute in the highest degree to their parents' welfare.[30]

Natural Fertility Awareness

The sexual activity, in which husband and wife are intimately and chastely united with one another, through which human life is transmitted, is, as the recent Council recalled, "noble and worthy." It does not, moreover, cease to be legitimate even when, for reasons independent of their will, it is foreseen to be infertile. For its natural adaptation to the expression and strengthening of the union of husband and wife is not thereby suppressed. The fact is, as experience shows, that new life is not the result of each and every act of sexual intercourse. God has wisely ordered laws of nature and the incidence of fertility in such a way that successive births are already naturally spaced through the inherent operation of these laws. The Church, nevertheless, in urging men to the observance of the precepts of the natural law, which it interprets by its constant doctrine, teaches that each and every marital act must of necessity retain its intrinsic relationship to the procreation of human life.[31]

Procreation and love

This particular doctrine, often expounded by the magisterium of the Church, is based on the inseparable connection, established by God, which man on his own initiative may not break, between the unitive significance and the procreative significance which are both inherent to the marriage act.

The reason is that the fundamental nature of the marriage act, while uniting husband and wife in the closest intimacy, also renders them capable of generating new life — and this as a result of laws written into the actual nature of man and of woman. And if each of these essential qualities, the unitive and the procreative, is preserved, the use of marriage fully retains its sense of true mutual love and its ordination to the supreme responsibility of parenthood to which man is called. We believe that our contemporaries are particularly capable of seeing that this teaching is in harmony with human reason.[32]

Give way to one another in obedience to Christ

Wives should regard their husbands as they regard the Lord.
As the Church submits to Christ,
so should wives to their husbands, in everything.
Husbands should love their wives
just as Christ loved the Church
And sacrificed himself for her to make her holy.
Husbands must love their wives
as they love their own bodies;
for a man to love his wife,
is for him to love himself. (*Eph* 5:21-28)

Praying for your Children

For our children

Father of mankind, you have given me these children, and entrusted them to my charge, to bring them up for you and to prepare them for everlasting life. Help me with your heavenly grace to fulfil this sacred duty. Teach me what to give, and what to withhold; when to reprove and when to forbear. Make me gentle, yet firm; considerate and watchful. Through Christ our Lord. Amen.

At the time of baptism

Father, in baptism you have likened this child of ours to Christ the Lord and made him (her) a member of your priestly people. Make him (her) a living offering pleasing to you so that he (she) may always belong to your family on earth and be a fellow-citizen of your saints in heaven. Through Christ our Lord. Amen.

At confirmation

Father, fulfill your promise, and send down on N. the Holy Spirit. Help him (her) bear witness before the world to the Gospel of Jesus Christ our Lord, who lives and reigns for ever and ever. Amen.

At first communion

Father, today, for the first time, you are calling our child N. to the table of the Eucharist. We ask you that he (she) may be a worthy member of Christ's mystical body, the Church. In the power of the Eucharist preserve him (her) from the assaults of evil, strengthen his (her) faith, and make him (her) a witness to your love. Through Christ our Lord. Amen.

Going to school

God our Saviour, you sat among the teachers of the law, listening to them and questioning them. We entrust our child to you while he (she) is at school. Fill him (her) with the spirit of wisdom; open his (her) mind so that he (she) may learn the knowledge necessary for this life and for the life to come. Help him (her) in all he (she) has to do. Give him (her) perseverance and strength; make him (her) responsive and hard-working. You are the way, the truth and the life; do not let him (her) be led astray from the right path by false teaching. May he (she) grow like you, Lord Jesus, in age, in wisdom, and in grace before God and men. Amen.

For the children's future

Lord, help our children to know the road you have chosen for them; may they give you glory and attain salvation. Sustain them with your strength, and let them not be satisfied with easy goals. Enlighten us, their parents that we may help them to recognise their calling in life and respond to it generously. May we put no obstacle in the way of your inner guidance. Amen.

For priestly vocation

Lord God, you provide the Church with those who work for the Gospel. If it be your will, sow in our family the seeds of a vocation; in our home may there be one who chooses as the ideal of his life to serve you in his brothers. Through Christ our Lord. Amen.

For young people

We commend all young people to you, Lord: children, teenagers and students; engaged and newly married couples, and young parents. Grant them health, wisdom, and the joy of living in your presence; and grant those who care for them, their leaders, teachers and counsellors, your spirit of understanding and love. Through Christ our Lord. Amen.

A parent's prayer

Heavenly Father, who loves all mankind as a father loves a child, be mindful of my children (*names*) and of their mother and father. Graciously protect them in all they do and help them to resist temptation. Grant for me, myself, to be so full of your loving grace that this will speak to them about you.

Provide for their needs in every way and protect them from all evil. Give them wisdom in a confused world and bless them to trust in Jesus in every way. Strengthen their guardian angels to protect them from harm, and bring them at last to your heavenly kingdom. Through Christ our Lord, Amen.

For a grown-up child

I call down the Lord's blessing upon you, my child. You have left home and are out there on your own.

May the Lord bless you as you awake in the morning and keep you safe this day in body, mind and spirit.

May he walk with you as I can no longer.

May he bless the places you live and work in, and show his loving concern, as I once did when I so often asked where you had been and with whom.

May he bless the roads you travel and all who travel with you.

May he bless your finances and teach you to be generous to those who have less than you.

May he lead you in truthful ways, reminding you to give always of your best and put others needs before your own.

May he teach you to forgive, as we often forgave one another... when you stumbled and I chided you, when I said 'no' and you did not understand.

May you be blessed with the knowledge of the love of God, guarding you and lighting the path before you as I am blessed in knowing that you are safe under the shadow of his wings.

May you grow in relationship with the Lord, being blessed in the certain knowledge that he will never fail in his love, never forsake you, and always be there to comfort.

May you be blessed in the knowledge that I do not worry because I know that you are safe in the hands of the only person I trust to love you more than I ever can. Amen.

Prayers for your Family

For the family

God our Father, source of all our family has and is, help us to follow the example of the family of your Son, the holy family of Nazareth. May we love one another as they did, and come to share eternal happiness with them in heaven. Through Christ our Lord. Amen.

Prayer for all your family

May God's will be done.
Be blessed for everything, O Lord;
and give me your pardon and your grace.
Bless my beloved ones, all of them;
grant to their souls conversion and holiness.
May my dear nephews and my niece
Be Christians and apostles.
Give your grace to the souls I love,
light and supernatural life to every soul.
Bless and guide your Church
and sanctify her priests,
my spiritual father among them.
And take me altogether to yourself,
in life, in death, and for eternity. Amen.[33]

Prayer of a father

Father, I thank you for the gift of my family for whom I now pray and upon whom I now ask you to shower your blessings. With St. Joseph as my guide, may I always be ready to spend my life for them.

Bless my wife whom you have given to me as my spouse, sharing in your wondrous work of creation. May I see her as my equal and treat her with the love of Christ for his Church. May Mary be her guide and help her to find your peace and your grace.

Bless my children with your life and presence. May the example of your son be the foundation upon which their lives are built, that the Gospel may always be their hope and support.

I ask you, Father, to protect and bless my family. Watch over it so that in the strength of your love its members may enjoy prosperity, possess the gift of your peace and, as the Church alive in our home, always bear witness to your glory in the world. Amen.[34]

Prayer of thanksgiving

Dear Lord, what gifts I have received from you! My hope of salvation, bought at such a price.

Your gift of yourself, hidden in bread and wine, open to me, despite the shallowness of my preparation and thanksgiving, at Mass. Your gift of forgiveness when I seek reconciliation for my sins.

Then, the gift of my family, of those I love most in the world. My parents, who nurtured me and loved me as Our Lady and St. Joseph nurtured and loved you in Palestine and are now, I pray, with you, whom they loved above all. The journey my husband and I have made together over many years, not always in harmony, but always coming back together, dissonance resolved. The exquisite excitement, pleasure and apprehension at the birth of our children! Watching their growing, their enthusiasms, their weaknesses, making us sometimes anxious, sometimes angry, often exhausted. How can I thank you enough for all this?

Now, our children undertake new roles. They are our supporters, as we grow older. Our grandchild brings us new delight – the unearned love that grandparents receive from a grandchild.

Dear Lord, the whole cycle of life is a beautiful gift. Humbly and inadequately, I thank you and pray that we may all grow in closeness to you, to our Heavenly Father and to the Holy Spirit.

For marriage and family

Our God, indivisible Trinity, you created the human being "in your image" and you admirably formed him as male and female that so together, united and in reciprocal collaboration with love, they fulfilled Your project of being fruitful.

We pray to You for all our families that so, finding in You their initial inspiration and model, that is fully expressed in the Holy Family of Nazareth, can live the human and Christian values that are necessary to consolidate and sustain their experience of love and to be the foundations of a more human and Christian basis of our society.

We pray to You and for the intercession of Mary, our Mother, and Saint Joseph. We ask this Jesus Christ our Lord. Amen.[35]

Prayer to the Sacred Heart

Sacred Heart of Jesus and Immaculate Heart of Mary, I come to you to consecrate myself and my entire family to your two hearts. I desire to renew the vows of my baptism and place each member of my family through an act of Faith, Hope and Love into loving union with the Holy Family of Jesus, Mary and Joseph. I dedicate myself and each member of my family to the Guardian Angels God has given each one of us. O Holy Guardian Angels, enlighten, guide and protect each one so as to lead us safely home to heaven.

At Fatima, dear Mother of God, you appeared with St. Joseph and the Child Jesus blessing the world. O Holy Family, bestow blessings upon me and my entire family so that we may live the Christ-life. I desire that each member of my family adore always the Most Blessed Trinity and love our God in the Most Blessed Sacrament. Grant peace to each member of my family. Keep each one in the grace of Jesus Christ. Never permit any of my family to stray from the true faith and for any member who has strayed, I beseech you to bind up the wounds, lift up the fallen, and keep each of our loved ones in grace. Bid them come back to their Father's true home. Amen.[36]

For relatives and friends

God our Father, look kindly on our relatives and friends. By the power of your Holy Spirit, pour out on them the gifts of your love. Give them health of mind and body, that they may love you with all their heart and do your will in all things. Through Christ our Lord. Amen.

Sacrament of Marriage

Like each of the seven sacraments, so also marriage is a real symbol of the event of salvation, but in its own way. "The spouses participate in it as spouses, together, as a couple, so that the first and immediate effect of marriage (*res et sacramentum*) is not supernatural grace itself, but the Christian conjugal bond, a typically Christian communion of two persons because it represents the mystery of Christ's incarnation and the mystery of His covenant. The content of participation in Christ's life is also specific: conjugal love involves a totality, in which all the elements of the person enter-appeal of the body and instinct, power of feeling and affectivity, aspiration of the spirit and of will. It aims at a deeply personal unity, the unity that, beyond union in one flesh, leads to forming one heart and soul; it demands indissolubility and faithfulness in definitive mutual giving; and it is open to fertility (cf *Humanae vitae*, 9). In a word it is a question of the normal characteristics of all natural conjugal love, but with a new significance which not only purifies and strengthens them, but raises them to the extent of making them the expression of specifically Christian values."[37]

Indissolubility

Conjugal communion is characterised not only by its unity but also by its indissolubility: "As a mutual gift of two persons, this intimate union, as well as the good of children, imposes total fidelity on the spouses and argues for an unbreakable oneness between them."

It is a fundamental duty of the Church to reaffirm strongly, as the Synod Fathers did, the doctrine of the indissolubility of marriage. To all those who, in our times, consider it too difficult, or indeed impossible, to be bound to one person for the whole of life, and to those caught up in a culture that rejects the indissolubility of marriage and openly mocks the commitment of spouses to fidelity, it is necessary to reconfirm the good news of the definitive nature of that conjugal love that has in Christ its foundation and strength.

Being rooted in the personal and total self-giving of the couple, and being required by the good of the children, the indissolubility of marriage finds its ultimate truth in the plan that God has manifested in His revelation: He wills and He communicates the indissolubility of marriage as a fruit, a sign and a requirement of the absolutely faithful love that God has for man and that the Lord Jesus has for the Church.[38]

Some Favourite Prayers

Day by Day

Thanks be to you, our Lord Jesus Christ,
for all the benefits which you have given us,
for all the pains and insults which you
have borne for us.
Most merciful Redeemer, Friend and Brother,
may we know you more clearly,
love you more dearly,
and follow you more nearly,
day by day. Amen.[39]

One day at a time

God, grant us the
Serenity to accept the things we cannot change,
Courage to change the things we can and
Wisdom to know the difference –
Living one day at a time;
Enjoying one moment at a time;
Accepting hardships
as the pathway to peace;
Taking, as He did, this sinful world
as it is, not as we would have it:

Trusting that He will make all things
right if we surrender to His will;
That we may be reasonably happy in this life
and supremely happy with Him
forever in the next. Amen.[40]

May we do your will

Teach us, good Lord,
to serve you as you deserve,
to give and not to count the cost,
to fight and not to heed the wounds,
to toil and not to seek for rest,
to labour and not to ask for any reward,
save that of knowing that we do your will. Amen.[41]

God alone suffices

Let nothing disturb you,
nothing affright you,
all things are passing
God never changes.
Patient endurance
attaineth to all things.
Who possesses God
in nothing is wanting
God alone suffices.[42]

Peace in our heart

Lead us from death to life,
from lies to truth.
Lead us from despair to hope,
from fear to trust.
Lead us from hatred to love,
from war to peace.
Let peace fill our heart,
our world,
our universe. Amen.[43]

St Michael's Prayer

Holy Michael the Archangel, defend us in the day of battle; be our safeguard against the wickedness and snares of the devil. May God rebuke him, we humbly pray: And do thou, Prince of the Heavenly Host, by the power of God thrust down to hell Satan and all wicked spirits, who wander throughout the world for the ruin of souls. Amen.

Learning to love

Lord, make us an instrument of thy peace;
where there is hatred, let us sow love;
where there is injury, pardon;
where there is doubt, faith;

where there is despair, hope;
where there is darkness, light;
and where there is sadness, joy.
O Divine Master,
grant that we may not so much seek
to be consoled as to console;
to be understood, as to understand;
to be loved, as to love;
for it is in giving that we receive,
it is in pardoning that we are pardoned,
and it is in dying that we are born to Eternal Life.
Amen.[44]

Prayer for parents

Father, it is your commandment that we should honour our father and mother; hear the prayers we offer you for them. Grant them many years on earth and keep them in health of mind and body. Bless their work and all they do. Give them back a hundred-fold whatever they have done for me. Inspire them with your love and help them to fulfil your holy law. One day, may I be their comfort and support, so that having enjoyed their affection on earth I may have the joy of being with them forever in your home in heaven. Through Christ our Lord. Amen.

Bless our work

Lord God, our Creator and our Father, from whom all good things come, we give you thanks for supporting us in our work, and for the knowledge, courage and honesty of our brothers and sisters, on whose work our life depends. We pray to you for our friends and companions, for those who direct our work and for those who work with us, especially for N. N. (*pause for silence*). We pray to you for the men and women who work in the factories, in the fields, in offices, on the roads and at home. Sustain mothers and fathers in their work and their cares; help them as they work for their families. Guide the young in their choice of vocation and profession. Bring health to the sick and comfort to the aged. By doing the work you have entrusted to us, may we serve you with joyful hearts and in a spirit of brotherly love. Amen.

For the sick

Father, your only Son took upon himself the sufferings and weakness of all mankind; through his passion and cross he taught us how good can be brought out of suffering. Look upon our brothers and sisters who are ill. In the midst of illness and pain, may they be united with Christ, who heals both body and soul; may they know the consolation promised to those who suffer and be fully restored to health. Through Christ our Lord. Amen.

For the suffering

Father, you are the unfailing refuge of those who suffer. Bring peace and comfort to the sick and the infirm, to the aged and the dying. Give all those who look after them knowledge, patience, and compassion. Inspire them with actions which will bring relief, words which will enlighten, and love which will bring comfort. We commend to you the disheartened, the rebellious, those torn by temptation or tormented by desire, and those wounded or abused by the ill will of men. Lord, pour out on us your Spirit of love, understanding and sacrifice; may we then give effective help to the suffering we meet on our way. Help us to answer their cry, for it is our own. Amen.

For the aged

Eternal Father, unchanged down the changing years, be near to those who are aged. Even though their bodies weaken, grant that their spirit may be strong; may they bear weariness and affliction with patience, and, at the end, meet death with serenity. Through Christ our Lord. Amen.

For the dying

All powerful and merciful Father in the death of Christ you have opened a gateway to eternal life. Look kindly on our brother (sister) N., who is suffering his (her) last agony. United to the passion and death of your Son, and saved by the blood he shed, may he (she) come before you with confidence. Through the same Christ our Lord. Amen.

Prayers for a journey

Lord, you fill every place with your presence: be with me on this journey. Help me reach my destination and bring me home safely and in good health. May my journey bring joy and encouragement to all I meet, a message of hope and a witness to the Christian life.

Father, grant us fair weather and a safe journey. In the company of your angel, may we arrive happily at our destination and come at the last to the gateway of eternal life. Through Jesus Christ our Lord. Amen.

Protect us as we journey

Lord God, guard us on the road we are about to take. Be with us in every need: our companion on the journey, our refreshment in heat, our protection from cold and rain, our support when tired, our encouragement in adversity, our strength when the going is hard, our port in shipwreck; under your guidance may we arrive happily at our destination and return safe and well to our homes. Through Christ our Lord. Amen.

In the difficulties of life

All-powerful and merciful Father, refreshment of the weary, comfort in sorrow, strength in our weakness, hear the prayer which we sinners make to you: save and sustain us in our present need, and help us to face the future with courage.

Father, you know our difficulties and our needs. In your love we can overcome all things; strengthen our confidence and our faith, and let us know your fatherly care.

Lord, grant us the grace to meet our tasks and responsibilities with calm and fortitude; consoled by you, help us bring encouragement to our brothers. Through Christ our Lord. Amen.

Lord you are our refuge

He who dwells in the shelter of the Most High
and abides in the shade of the Almighty
says to the Lord: "My refuge,
my stronghold, my God in whom I trust!"

It is he who will free you from the snare
of the fowler who seeks to destroy you;
he will conceal you under his pinions
and under his wings you will find refuge.
You will not fear the terror of the night
nor the arrow that flies by day,
nor the plague that prowls in the darkness
nor the scourge that lays waste at noon.

A thousand may fall at your side,
ten thousand at your right,
you, it will never approach;
his faithfulness is buckler and shield.

Your eyes have only to look
to see how the wicked are repaid,
you will have said: "Lord, my refuge!"
and have made the Most High your dwelling.

Upon you no evil shall fall,
no plague approach where you dwell.

For you has he commanded his angels,
to keep you in all your ways.

They shall bear you upon their hands
lest you strike your foot against a stone.
On the lion and the viper you will tread
and trample the young lion and the dragon.

His love he set on me, so I will rescue him;
protect him for he knows my name.
When he calls I shall answer: "I am with you."
I will save him in distress and give him glory.

With length of life I will content him;
I shall let him see my saving power.[45]

Endnotes

[1] From the Marriage Rite

[2] Meditation on marriage read out to every Catholic couple in the US before they exchanged wedding vows - (until 1969)

[3] *Lumen Gentium*, 11

[4] From the Marriage Rite

[5] From the Marriage Rite

[6] From the Marriage Rite

[7] From the Marriage Rite

[8] Nuptial Blessing from the Marriage Rite

[9] *Gaudium et Spes*, 48

[10] *Gaudium et Spes*, 48

[11] *Gaudium et Spes*, 48

[12] *Gaudium et Spes*, 48

[13] Nuptial Blessing from the Marriage Rite

[14] Extract from Pope John Paul II's prayer to Our Lady of Guadalupe, Protectress of the Unborn

[15] *www.CelebrateLove.co.uk*

[16] *www.CelebrateLove.co.uk*

[17] Book of Tobit, chapters 7 and 8

[18] Book of Tobit, chapters 7 and 8

[19] From the Song of Songs

[20] From the Song of Songs

[21] *Gaudium et Spes*, 50

[22] *Gaudium et Spes*, 51

[23] *www.catholic.org/prayers*

[24] Marriage blessing prayer *www.catholicdoors.com*

[25] Adapted from *www.CelebrateLove.co.uk*

[26] Diary entry, March 6 1912, from the Journal of Elisabeth Leseur, praying for the conversion of her atheist husband. After her death he returned to the practice of his faith and became a priest

[27] *Humanae Vitae*, 9

[28] *Humanae Vitae*, 9

[29] *Humanae Vitae*, 9

[30] *Humanae Vitae*, 9

[31] *Humanae Vitae*, 11

[32] *Humanae Vitae*, 12

[33] Prayer of Elisabeth Leseur, April 9, 1911

[34] *www.catholic.org/prayers*

[35] Adapted from the official prayer of the VI World Meeting of Families Mexico 2009, http://www.wmf2009.com/esp/013oracion.htm

[36] *www.catholicparents.org*

[37] *Familiaris Consortio*, 13

[38] *Familiaris Consortio*, 13

[39] St Richard of Chichester

[40] Adapted from Pastor Reinhold Niebuhr's prayer.

[41] St Ignatius of Loyola

[42] St Teresa of Avila

[43] Adapted from Blessed Mother Teresa of Calcutta's Peace Prayer

[44] Adapted from St Francis of Assisi's prayer

[45] Psalm 91.